Jesus My Everything

Jesus My Everything

Bonita L. Williams

VISION INSPIRED
PUBLICATIONS
Let your words take flight

Atlanta, Georgia

Jesus My Everything

Bonita L. Williams

Vision Inspired Publications
Atlanta, GA

Copyright © 2016 Bonita L. Williams

ISBN: **0-9856187-8-7**

ISBN-13: **978-0-9856187-8-0**

Published by Vision Inspired Publications

PRINTED IN THE UNITED STATES OF AMERICA

Dedication

This book is dedicated to everyone who has accepted the gift of salvation from our Lord and Savior Jesus Christ

CONTENTS

Acknowledgement

Note from Author

CONTENTS

ACKNOWLEDGMENT

Jesus My Everything

The wonder- working power of God is amazing. The poems and reflections contained in this book are all God inspired. I have been blessed by God to experience His unconditional love. It is my prayer that something contained on the pages of this book will draw you closer to our Lord and Savior Jesus Christ.

NOTE FOR AUTHOR

As we travel on this journey called life it is imperative that we keep our focus on Jesus. Everything we need from here to Heaven has already been made available to us through the death, burial and resurrection of our Lord and Savior. We can celebrate daily as we reflect on God's graciousness toward us. EVERYTHING we will ever need has already been made available for us. Before we were knitted in our mothers' womb God knew us. Each day new mercies are given to us. I have come to appreciate each comma of my life. I used to live from day to day and then I went from moment to moment. I am now living comma to comma. We never know what will happen. Life is a fleeting blur at times. Holding on to God's unchanging hand allows us to weather any storm, any trial or any circumstance that we face.

Bonita L. Williams

Jesus My Everything

The Tiny Bundle

Hope, joy, peace, love all wrapped in a
tiny bundle.

Gently placed in a manger on a stable's
floor,

The tiny bundle holding all of our
redemption and so much more.

A bundle from Heaven to show us our
Father's care

Offering salvation to people everywhere.

Joy to the world wrapped in a tiny bundle.

Extreme Sacrifice

Guiltless, blameless, He who knew no sin

took all my sin's burdens to the cross.

Holy, righteous, total deity offered His

blood on Calvary for those that are lost.

Marvelous, wonderful, Prince of Peace,

sacrificed His life to reconcile our souls.

The true depth of His love will take a

lifetime to be told.

All honor, all glory, and all majesty to

Him we owe.

Oh what an extreme sacrifice was made

because He loves us so.

Be Still and Know that God IS GOD

While trying to keep up with the pace of the race, we often fail to stop and consider just which direction we are travelling.

Will our present path lead to success or failure?

How can we be sure?

How do we know that the choices we make are the right ones?

The answer to our quest is to rely on the problem solver (God).

Standing firm on His promises we can be assured of His love for us.

Acknowledging that God has everything under control allows us to rest safely in His arms.

STOP-KNOW-ACKNOWLEDGE-
BELIEVE

God is GOD

He is able to do far more than we can ever
begin to imagine.

Trust Him

Accept His unconditional love

Enjoy fellowship with Him

Enter into His presence with thanksgiving
and praise.

Be still and know that God is GOD.

My Shero

Never made the headlines of the

newspaper

Name not listed in WHO's WHO

Mantle not full of trophies

Walls not covered with plaques.

Never recognized for outstanding

performances

Not named Woman on the Year.

Doesn't run in the most popular circles

Not known as a fashion icon.

Not sought after for public appearances

So just what make her so special

Warm smile

Caring heart

Loving nature

Giving of herself in every way serving as a living example of God's Word through her loving spirit.

The Ability of God

God, I asked if you could hear me

because the way out I could not see.

Every door seemed to be closing in my

face

I panicked because I forgot about your

amazing grace.

Father, the enemy wanted me to believe

that all was lost.

He wanted me to forget the cost you paid

to set me free.

The enemy wanted me to struggle with

doubt.

He wanted me to believe that you would

not bring me out.

He tried to rob me of my peace by trying

to convince me that the storm would not

cease.

Oh, but thank you Heavenly Father for the truth that you are able to bring me through every trial and every storm.

When I put my trust in you there is no reason for alarm.

You are my lawyer in the court room, my doctor in a sick room,

the writer of checks from your Heavenly bank account,

strength when I am weak,

mover of mountains.

You and you alone God have the ability to keep me.

.

God's Faithfulness

In the valley of despair

on the mountain high

Where ever we find ourselves God is

there.

Late in the midnight hours when all seems

lost

when pain racks our body

God is there.

Tears seem like they will near cease

God is there.

On our best behavior or if we are wretches

undone

God is there.

Consistent is His love for us

Faithful is our God in every situation.

Faithful is His love

Faithful is His grace and mercy

Faithful when we are not

Faithful when we honor Him

Faithful when we don't

Faithful is our God

God faithfully meets all of our needs.

Love Sustains Me

In despair loves sustains me

On the mountain high love sustains me

Misery knocking at my door love sustains
me

Searching for the answer love sustains me

Shouting halleluiah love sustains me

Feeling weighed down by the enemy's
attack love sustains me

Basking in God's grace because His love
sustains me.

Needing My Shepherd

A sheep astray at times I seem to be

Wandering wild and free

Needing the my Shepherd to rescue me

Unaware of the perils that lay ahead

Oblivious to the path I will tread.

Needing my Shepherd to be in my stead.

Hurt on the journey from the enemy's

attack

Not safe from the wolves I attract

Needing my Shepard to guard and protect

Needing my Shepherd who knows the

way,

Needing my Shepherd who is with me

each day.

For Me

For me, He came from Heaven above to allow me to experience God's grace and love.

For me, He hung upon the tree

For me, He bled at Calvary

For me, He paid the price for sin and iniquity

For me, He died so that I could have victory.

For me, He rose with all power in His hand.

For me, He came so that I can stand.

For me! For me! Yes! He did it all for me!

Calvary

Meek and lowly, humble and pure

Willing and ready His purpose was sure.

Ransom the souls that once were lost.

He bled and died upon the cross.

For no crimes of His own did He hang on

that tree.

Oh No! Not for Him, it was all done for

you and me.

The agony He suffered was the price that

He paid.

So that the way to Heaven for all believers

was made.

Amazing Wonderfully Amazing

I heard them say that you would always
make a way.

They said all they had to do was pray.

I heard them say you would take away the
pain; that you had cleansed them from all
their guilt and stains.

I heard them say that you were the doctor
in a sick room and the lawyer in a
courtroom.

I heard them say that you were always
there.

I heard them say that you are everywhere.

One day when the load had gotten too
much for me to bear, I decided to see if
you would even care. I fell down on my
knees. And said Lord oh Lord please.

Your Spirit gently spoke to me "My child
be at ease."
You took away my guilt and shame and
told me I was no longer the same.
Your blood cleansed me through and
through and I know I belong to you.
Now just like them I can truly say that you
are amazing
Wonderfully Amazing.

Much Love
(A godly mother)

Didn't understand all the ways you

showed your love.

The strict rules. The no nonsense

expectations you had.

The "My way or the highway" attitude

seemed very harsh.

The insistence that only my best would do

was often a challenge to understand.

The unwavering desire for me to stay on

the right road.

The relentless attempts to keep order no

matter the cost.

The mothering that sometimes felt like

smothering.

Your persistence, your determination, and your zeal were all measures of your love for me.

My Anchor

Tossed to and fro on the stormy sea of life,

Sometimes experiencing grief and strife

No land in sight as I can see

Wondering if I will ever break free.

Remembering my anchor, my strong hold

Gives me comfort no matter how old.

Assured of His presence no matter the

tide.

I find great peace when in the Lord I

abide.

Our Shepherd

All we like sheep sometimes lose our way.

No matter how we try not to, we still may stray.

It's wonderful to know in times like that our Shepherd knows the way.

He finds the still waters that we can rest beside.

Resting in the green pastures that He will provide.

He searches our souls and restores us.

He protects us from the dangers that surround us.

He heals our wounds.

He showers us with His blessings.

His grace and His mercy carries us each and every day.

He promises us that He will be with us

forever.

In His perfect care we can always stay.

What I Believe

I believe Jesus shed His blood for me.

He bore the cross so that I could me free.

I believe that a home is Heaven is mine all mine.

It was purchased by my Savior divine.

I believe that love, joy and peace belong to me.

I believe that I already have the victory.

I believe that one day Jesus will come for me and then I will live with Him for eternity.

Never Forsaken

I read a promise made by the Lord.

He promised never to forsake me, never to

leave me alone.

He promised to be with me through thick

and thin.

He promised to help no matter what state

I find myself in.

High on the mountain top, low in the

valley, bubbling with joy, tears that seem

never to stop.

No matter the problem He is always there

to solve them.

No matter the pain my hand He holds.

No matter the age, no matter how old.

He's promised to keep me and never leave

me alone.

I hold tightly to this promise for with each passing day.

He shows me His love even when I stray.

He's made a way out of no way for me, He given me joy.

He's set me free.

Never forsaken -no never alone, He's always with me on this journey to my Heavenly home.

Gratitude

Gratitude should be the attitude that we
daily embrace
Always remembering to thank God for
His amazing grace.
A heart full of THANK YOU to God for
always making a way.
Grateful for how He sustains us each and
every day.
Lips full of praise singing of His glory
Willing always to share the redemption
story.
Hands raised in adoration to the one true
God of every nation.
Glory, honor, and ultimate praise-- songs
of gratitude for the rest of our days.

Following Jesus

Where you lead me I will follow.

Where you guide me I will go.

I will daily follow your instructions

because I know you love me so!

Your plans for me are not always clear,

But I don't worry because you are always

near.

There is no need to be frustrated or sit

around with doubt

Instead of hearing grumbling and

complaining, from me you'll receive a

victory shout.

I remember what you did for me when

you hang on Calvary.

The sacrifice you made to set my soul free.

Yes, precious Savior where you lead me I

will follow

where you guide me I will go

I will daily follow your instructions

because you love me so!

Mindful Praise

Lord, am I thinking of you right now or
am I allowing the cares of this world to
drown you out?

Am I truly acting in faith or am I dealing
in doubt?

Do I begin each day sure of your amazing
grace or do I fill my time trying to run at
my own pace?

Do I truly believe that you know what's
best for me or do I spend my time looking
at only what I can see?

Lord, I want to offer you mindful praise.

Praise and worship to you for the rest of
my days.

Praising you no matter what I go through

Praising you for what I know is true.

Praising you for your everlasting love.

Love that is showered on me from above.

Lord, I purpose in my heart this very day

to praise you regardless of what comes my

way.

The Invitation

I received an invitation given personally
to me.

The invitation stated that with its
acceptance I would be made free.

I didn't have to get all cleaned up or act a
certain way.

In fact the invitation told be exactly what
to say.

This sounds too good to be true was the
thought that came to me.

Someone offered to pay my sin debt so
that I could be set free.

Someone died for my sins on an old
rugged cross.

Someone sacrificed their life so that my
soul would not be lost.

I was astonished by the fact of such an
unselfish act.
And even though I had trouble believing
this could be true
I decided to try what I was told to do.
I prayed a prayer of repentance using the
words in my heart that I heard.
Asking for forgiveness and receiving
cleansing by Jesus' blood.
I chose to accept the gift of eternal life
being offered to me
Now I live each day knowing that I am
able walk in total victory.

The Joy Within

The sun's not shining outside the door.

The grass doesn't seem greener any more.

The laughter seems to have ceased.

The pain and strife is on the increase.

Problem after problem seems to be calling.

From the mountain you seem to be falling.

From all accounts you should be in
despair.

But somehow you seem to have joy from
somewhere.

Why, isn't your head hung low in
distress?

Why aren't you breaking under all the
stress?

How can you smile when I know what
you are going through?

Why haven't all these problems affected
you?
Tell me what helps you make it from day
to day?
Please tell me what you have to say?

Our Provider

There is not a need that He won't meet

Not an obstacle He can't defeat

Not a way that He can't make

Not one promise will He break.

Safe and secure in His love

Blessings are showered on us from above.

Trusting, believing that His Word is true

Knowing always He will bring us

through.

Only You

What would my life be without you?

How could I make it through if you were

not there to guide me?

Where could I run to in my time of

distress?

Who would love me like you do?

How would I be able to stand?

Who would keep me clothed and in my

right mind?

When I cried out who would answer?

When the tears flowed down my cheeks

who would wipe them away?

Who can mend a broken heart?

Who can scatter the darkness and bring

forth the light?

It's YOU dear LORD only YOU!!!

Waiting

Patiently waiting for me to yield to His will.

Waiting for me to finally be still.

Waiting for me to rest in His grace.

Waiting for me to run in the race.

Not parked on the sidelines hoping to start, but running the race with love in my heart.

Waiting to hear the words that I say.

Waiting to answer when I choose to pray.

Waiting for me to let go of the fear.

Waiting for me to realize that He is always near.

Waiting for me to trust His plan.

Waiting for me to reach for His hand.

Waiting for me to be done with myself.

Waiting, just waiting on me.

Peace

Peace, dear God you give to me in my
times of despair,
A sweet and gentle reminder that you are
always there.
When the storms are raging and life's
billows are tossing me to and fro.
It is comforting to know that to you I can
go.
Trusting you to guide me in whatever
comes my way,
Aware that I'm in your presence each and
every day.
Peace flowing like a river to calm my
restless soul
Assurance of knowing that you are in total
control.

Oh! Jesus

So great is your love for me.

So amazing is your care for me.

Impossible to comprehend just how deep
your love goes.

You shed your blood to save my soul.

Day by day you keep me.

Moment by moment you guide me.

Great is your love towards me.

You comfort me in my darkest hour.

You wipe all my tears away.

You give me your strength in my time of
weakness.

You are my shelter during every storm.

You are the anchor that holds me when
life is tossing me to and fro.

You are the hiding place I can run to no matter what life brings my way. Jesus you are my EVERYTHING!

ABOUT AUTHOR

Bonita L. Williams, a generational author, is a servant of God, whose passion is spreading the Good News of the Gospel of Jesus Christ with all she meets. Her greatest desire is to utilize her God given gifts to make a positive difference in the lives of others. She is a Bible teacher, workshop facilitator, empowerment seminar leader, and a conference speaker who has committed her life to instructing, inspiring and encouraging women of faith.

ALSO BY BONITA L WILLIAMS

Dear Daughters

The book focuses on our relationship with God. It provides activities which allow readers to spend time daily with God.

His Daughters: Leaning and Depending on the Lord

The book focuses on the source of our strength Jesus. It provides the readers with exercises which aid in the development of a closer walk with our Lord and Savior.

Saved Daughters: Waiting until Jesus Comes

The book contains God inspired letters as well as spiritual lessons learned from ten biblical women.

A Well- Watered Garden

Bonita Williams' sincere and deeply touching collection of poetry chronicles some of the important events and special times in her life. Readers will find a variety of God inspired poems which are moving and thought provoking.

Preparing to Witness

Book contains lessons which focus on the "Great Commission "given to us by God. The activities provide readers with useful techniques for witnessing.

And Still I Praise

The book offers readers an opportunity to spend time with God daily through journaling experiences.

www.ingramcontent.com/pod-product-compliance
Lightning Source LLC
Chambersburg PA
CBHW071024040426
42443CB00007B/923